WITHDRAWN

LIGHTNING
BOLT
BOOKS™

Brown Everywhere

Kristin Sterling

Lerner Publications Company
Minneapolis

Lerner Publications Company
A division of Lerner Publishing Group, Inc.
241 First Avenue North
Minneapolis, MN 55401 U.S.A.

Website address: www.lernerbooks.com

Library of Congress Cataloging-in-Publication Data

Sterling, Kristin.
   Brown everywhere / by Kristin Sterling.
       p. cm. — (Lightning bolt books.™— Colors everywhere)
   Includes index.
   ISBN 978-0-7613-5438-3 (lib. bdg. : alk. paper)
   1. Brown—Juvenile literature. 2. Colors—Juvenile literature. I. Title.
   QC495.5.S744   2011
   535.6—dc22   2009044914

Manufactured in the United States of America
1 — CG — 7/15/10

Contents

The Color Brown

Do you like warm, natural colors? Many people love the color brown.

This chess board is brown.

Look around you.
Brown is everywhere!

Things that are made of wood are often brown. **Choo-Choo!** A train zips along a wooden track.

A family sits on a wooden bench at a park. They enjoy spending a day outside.

This brown wooden bench makes a good resting spot.

7

Animals of all sizes are brown.

Ben's horse has a silky brown coat.

A hedgehog is a small brownish animal. It rolls into a tight ball when it is scared.

Hedgehogs can also run, climb, and swim.

Many things that we eat and drink are brown. You can make sandwiches with whole wheat bread.

Whole wheat bread is light brown.

Hot chocolate is a
tasty drink on cold days.

More marshmallows
please!

11

Brown is a common eye color. This boy has sparkling brown eyes.

Many people also have brown hair. Aaliyah's hair is brown and curly.

Aaliyah likes wearing brown clothes that match her dark curls.

Shades of Brown

Brown comes in many shades. The shades range from light to dark.

Different kinds of chocolate are often different shades of brown.

Khaki is a light brown color.

This naughty little puppy is khaki.

Ginger is a reddish brown color.

Julia's mom braids her
long ginger hair.

Umber is a medium brown color. Grizzly bears stay warm in their thick umber fur.

Grizzly bears live in the northwestern United States.

Brown and You

How do you feel about the color brown? Do you wear brown clothes?

Some people think brown is a
wholesome, earthy color.
It reminds them of nature.

What do you see
in nature that is
brown?

Other people think brown is dull. They think it is not as exciting as red, blue, or yellow.

Bella prefers bright colors to brown. She loves colorful balloons.

Do you think brown is comforting or boring?

Bernardo Loves Brown

Bernardo loves brown! It is his favorite color.

He has big brown eyes and straight brown hair. So does his brother!

Violins can be different shades of brown. They may be tan, dark brown, or reddish.

Bernardo plays the violin.

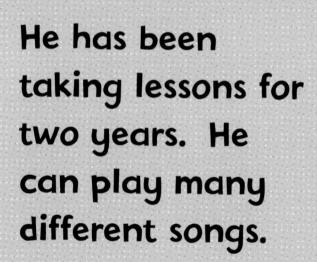

He has been taking lessons for two years. He can play many different songs.

His family has a brand-new
brown horse.

Bernardo feeds him every day.

Chocolate ice cream is
Bernardo's favorite dessert.

His brother likes it too!

what is your favorite color?

Fun Facts

- You can make brown paint by mixing together other paint colors like blue and orange, yellow and purple, or red and green.

- Many musical instruments are brown because they are made of wood. Some examples are violins, cellos, and guitars.

- Brownies are delicious desserts made with chocolate.

- Grizzly bears are also called brown bears. They eat plants and animals. They sleep through the winter to save energy.

- Farmland is covered by dark brown soil. Soil is dirt. Most of the food we eat is grown in soil.

- Brown dwarfs are objects in outer space. They are larger than planets but smaller than stars.

- Brown University is a college in Providence, Rhode Island.

- Baseball gloves are usually made of brown leather. They protect players' hands from injury. The first baseball gloves were worn in the 1870s.

Glossary

coat: an animal's fur

comforting: a word to describe something that eases troubles or cheers people up

dull: boring, not interesting

injury: damage or harm

shade: the darkness or lightness of a color

wholesome: healthful or good for the mind, the body, or the spirit

Further Reading

Bauer, Marion Dane. *One Brown Bunny.* New York: Orchard Books, 2009.

Enchanted Learning: Brown
http://www.enchantedlearning.com/colors/brown.shtml

Iyengar, Malathi Michelle. *Tan to Tamarind: Poems about the Color Brown.* San Francisco: Children's Book Press, 2009.

Martin, Bill, Jr. *Brown Bear, Brown Bear, What Do You See?* New York: Henry Holt, 2010.

Ross, Kathy. *Kathy Ross Crafts Colors.* Minneapolis: Millbrook Press, 2003.

Index

Photo Acknowledgments

The images in this book are used with the permission of: © Wolandmaster/ Dreamstime.com, p. 1; © Paul Burns/Digital Vision/Getty Images, p. 2; © Stock4B/Getty Images, p. 4; © Radius Images/Getty Images, pp. 5, 16; © Image Source/Getty Images, p. 6; © Kablonk/SuperStock, p. 7; © Fancy/Alamy, p. 8; © Nick Garbutt/NHPA/ Photoshot, p. 9; © Peter Cade/Digital Vision/Getty Images, p. 10; © BLOOMimage/Getty Images, p. 11; © Ryan McVay/Getty Images, p. 12; © Gary John Norman/The Image Bank/Getty Images, p. 13; © Danilo Ascione/Dreamstime.com, p. 14; © Lightly Salted/ Alamy, p. 15; © Photodisc/Getty Images, p. 17; © Ben Molyneux People/Alamy, p. 18; © John Lund/Sam Diephuis/Blend Images/Getty Images, p. 19; © fStop/SuperStock, p. 20; © Brad Wilson/Photographer's Choice/Getty Images, p. 21; © Sonya Etchison/ Shutterstock Images, pp. 22, 23, 25; © Gavril Margittai/Dreamstime.com, p. 24; © Lana Langlois/Dreamstime.com, p. 26; © Claudia Gopperl/Getty Images, p. 27; © James Baigrie/Riser/Getty Images, p. 28; Courtesy John Deere & Company, p. 29; © Ghislain & Marie David de Lossy/Stone/Getty Images, p. 30; © Stock Connection/SuperStock, p. 31.

Front cover: © Tan Wei Ming/Dreamstime.com (cello); © Paul Souders/Photodisc/Getty Images (bear); © Trinacria Photo/Shutterstock Images (football); © Todd Strand/ Independent Picture Service (toy cabin); © Thomas M Perkins/Shutterstock Images (ice cream cone); © Photodisc/Getty Images. (pine cones).